To Chari...
Best wishes
in all you do

tHrOuGH the FOG

A MEMOIR

A MOTHER AND HER SON'S
40 YEAR JOURNEY
WITH AUTISM

Thank you

Klara J. Co...

tHROuGH the FOG

A MEMOIR

A MOTHER AND HER SON'S
40 YEAR JOURNEY
WITH AUTISM

GLORIA JEAN COX

LANGDON STREET PRESS
212 3RD AVENUE NORTH, SUITE 290
MINNEAPOLIS, MN 55401
612.455.2293
WWW.LANGDONSTREETPRESS.COM

ISBN - 978-1-934938-57-7
ISBN - 1-934938-57-2
LCCN - 2010925041

COVER DESIGN BY ALAN PRANKE
TYPESET BY JAMES ARNESON

PRINTED IN THE UNITED STATES OF AMERICA

T.C., I dedicate this book to you.
And I thank you for dedicating yourself to me
and to the family we built together.
I am both honored and humbled by your selflessness
and your contribution to the woman,
sister, wife, and mother I have grown into today.
Thank you for a lifetime.

ACKNOWLEDGEMENTS

I must first thank God for his tender mercy.

To all my children—Bill, Scott, Kenny, Gregory, Jamala, Katari, and Me-Ling: I thank you for being my motivation.

I am grateful to my grandchildren, my nieces, and my nephews for keeping me young. Even when I've tried to take the easy way out, they never let me.

To Louisa, Tre', Rick, Dina, and the many other friends and fantastic people God has put into my life; to those of you I have known longer than I can remember; to those of you whom I have been blessed to find later in life; and to all of you who were there for me for no more than a passing moment: you held me up along the way, one and all.

To Staci and dear Molly, for never letting me lose focus of the big picture: I thank you for walking with me on this journey and making this book *our* goal, not just my own.

To my angel Arnetta, her husband, and their children: I thank God every day for sending you to me.

To my brother-in-law, for encouraging me, even when you didn't realize that's what you were doing: your honest words were sometimes what lifted me to the next level.

To my only sister, who pushed me to write these words: this experience turned into something that has brought the entire family closer. Not only has this taught me about them and their separate journeys, but it has allowed them to see me in a different light. I thank you for helping me write the story of my life and for making me believe my experiences were worthy enough to share.

To Jennifer and Shane: when you read these pages, I want you to be sure, without a shadow of a doubt, that there is a way *Through the Fog*, and you will find it.

FOREWORD

My sister is older than I am, so I have never known life without her by my side, helping me through every obstacle I have had to face, as I've tried to do the same for her.

There have been only a few times in our sixty-some years on Earth when we didn't live in the same apartment, in the same building, or on the same city block.

We have raised our families together, gone through both good times and bad with one another, and have been there to balance each other when we needed it most, even when separated during my constant excursions into the outside world.

Our separate journeys have taken us both down roads the other was not always able to follow. We have each had to deal with issues the other never had to face. It was these moments—when we were unable to stand shoulder to shoulder or look into each other's eyes and say, "I understand how you feel. I know what you are going through, and I am here for you, sister"—that were the most challenging for us. These were also the times that forced us to grow the most and to lean on our faith and what our great-grandmother instilled in us: *stick together, no matter what.*

This book is one of those moments for her.

My sister and I are complete opposites in many ways, which I believe is one of the reasons we balance each other so perfectly.

I am open, calling myself out before anyone else can, putting my own faults out there for the world to see, and not just owning them but standing on them, as if to stake my claim. This is how I start the communication that I believe is the first step to finding resolution.

My sister is quiet; she internalizes most things and gracefully, quietly finds just the right moment to begin communication that will lead her to the same place—resolution.

There are times when I need to be more of who my sister is, and she needs to be more of who I am to get the most growth and—sometimes—the best results possible.

It can be challenging to go outside our comfort zones, to push ourselves beyond our own limitations and to discover those things of which we are actually capable.

This is what I did for my sister with this book. I pushed her to write these words. I went beyond being supportive; I was relentless. I knew what she needed, even if she didn't know herself, just as she has known so many times before about me.

This journey she took, as a mother of a child with autism, was one she had to take alone.

I wanted to help her more. I wanted so badly to relieve her of some of the weight put on her in those years of not having answers and the guilt that came with so many decisions that she made for the benefit of her children.

No matter what my desire was for my sister, no matter how much support, understanding, love, and even money I could share with her, I could not give her the serenity that telling her story would bring to her life; I knew this to be true.

I knew that revisiting these memories, which at the time were so difficult to face, and remembering the decisions that in the moment seemed impossible for any loving mother to make would ultimately set her free.

I knew this because when I am blessed with the opportunity to look back at a situation, forty or more years after the fact, I see it so clearly. I see my mistakes, as well as my accomplishments. I am even able to forgive myself for any missteps, and on the best of days, I am proud of what I was able to get through, without knowing then what I know now.

I knew in my heart that with the gift of time, my sister would be able to step out of herself and be able to see the same picture that everyone around her has seen all along.

She would understand that what she was able to come through was one of the greatest accomplishments of her life, and that rather than feeling shame in it, she should feel great pride.

I could see it in her eyes as she shared with me the pieces of her story that she had forgotten so many years earlier. I could feel it in her energy each time we visited, throughout the process of her writing her memoir, and I read it on every page of this book—when I am able to see through my own tears.

I am grateful to my older sister for allowing me to push her into this project. I am proud of her for the contribution she has made by opening herself up for all of us to connect to her journey as a woman, a wife, a sister, a mother.

I am honored that she has allowed me to share in her laughter and tears and to have been able to be there to support her through both joy and sorrow.

I hope in reading these chapters of my sister's life, you will find some part of yourself in her strength, in her integrity, in her mistakes, and in her greatest accomplishments.

I hope her story inspires you, as it has me and the rest of our family.

I believe that whether or not you are on a similar journey, these pages will serve as medicine for you when you need it most.

Peace, love, and blessings,
Afeni Shakur-Davis

PROLOGUE

Atlanta, Georgia
Ocotober 10, 2007

Greg sat at the head of the table. Though his posture not typically erect, today he was sitting at full attention, very eager to dive into the cake that had been placed before him. His flitted from one thing to the next, while he used his two index fingers to conduct the Lesane-Cox rendition of "Happy Birthday." There were two cakes, one chocolate and one yellow, each with "Happy Birthday, Greg" in frosting across the top.

As we sang the last note of the song, Greg picked up a fork and a plate.

"Wait!" I called out. "Let's take a picture!" I had to capture this on film. Moments of my family's being together were not rare, but the atmosphere was different this day. Greg's turning forty was a big deal for all of us.

Greg's brothers and sister and their families gathered around him. Through the lens, I saw each of my children's eyes as they waited for me to take the picture. Greg's I could not see. His gaze was disconnected, his glance distant—it was anywhere except at the camera. I instructed everyone to say cheese.

"*Cheese!*" they all complied.

I knew Greg could not actually say "cheese," but I laughed inside as I saw him look around the room and then make the sign for "smile."

As Greg devoured his cake, his siblings continued to acknowledge him with hugs or friendly handshakes. Greg, as usual, paid almost no attention to them. I watched everyone attempt to engage him with happy birthday wishes. They tried a little harder this year because it was his fortieth. He only partially acknowledged them. Instead, he continued to eat his cake contentedly, closing out the world in which his family resided and finding comfort in his own.

CHAPTER ONE

My Three Sons

Today, when I think about what it took to survive my own choices, I am incredulous. The choice to marry young. Very young. The choice to conceive not one child but two, while I was still a teen. To have four more children all before I was twenty-five years old. These were decisions that designed my character, shaped my life, and led me to the settled and complete feeling I now enjoy.

The Bronx
November 1967

I cannot believe that my reflection in the mirror did not stop me in my tracks. I was only twenty-three, but I felt more like fifty-three. I had no time to connect to the whirlwind that my life had become. In retrospect, I'm grateful for not seeing it in that moment. If I had, I'd have noticed that I'd felt as if I were a woman walking through a windstorm. There are many simple things that we, as women, do for ourselves—iron our clothes, shop for a new pair of shoes, get our hair done—forget it; I had no time for any of these luxuries. I was so overwhelmed, I couldn't find myself. I asked myself why I felt so haggard, even though I knew the answer. But before I had time to conjure up a master plan, to smooth out the wrinkles both in my dress and in my life, one of my babies began to cry. I took a deep breath, gave myself one last glance, and turned to pick him up.

I was inside my tenement apartment on 158th Street between Melrose and Courtland in the South Bronx, carrying my youngest child around our 700-square-foot living space. The apartment had two bedrooms, but we'd converted it into three. Carefully balancing the baby, I picked up baby bottles and toys, as well as the dirty diapers from the morning that I hadn't had time to throw into the garbage. I was making my rounds as if I were a registered nurse, ensuring that my patients were happy and taken care of—except that my "patients" were my babies.

I had given birth three times in four years—all boys. There were very few moments to sit back and relish the new motherhood in which I'd wrapped myself. Diapers. Formula. Piles of laundry. Figuring out how to stretch the little money I had. More diapers. Still, I loved my children more than I'd loved anything in my life. As I kissed them, hugged them, and smelled them, I cherished every ounce of love I had for them with all my might. But before I'd even finished my teenage years, this new motherhood had spun my life out of control, not with one newborn, not with two, but with three sons, all under the age of four. When my first, Billy, was born on August 31, 1963, I had just turned eighteen. Scott was born just a year later on October 31, 1964. We welcomed our third son, Kenny, on November 10, 1966, when I was just six months shy of my twentieth birthday.

Though I didn't know it back then, this was around the time I began dying. Dying inside. Emotionally dying. I had no plan. No time to think about a plan. All I had were hungry mouths to feed.

Let me make it clear that with the birth of each child, I experienced a joy to which nothing could compare. But the joy of bearing my children and holding them and gazing into their newborn eyes was eclipsed by the overwhelming responsibilities of providing for them—that, and the responsibilities of maintaining a one-sided, futile marriage. Because my husband, Bill, didn't contribute financially or with his responsibilities as a father, the gradual effects of doing everything on my own caused the slow, quiet death of my spirit.

I remember the night when Bill came home and announced he'd accepted a new job. I eagerly waited for him to give me the details. Mostly, I wanted to know when he would be starting and when he'd get his first paycheck. We were poor. Very poor. So poor that we'd sometimes eat butter sandwiches because there was nothing else in the house.

"I'm going to be working at the Ford Motor Company," he told me.

"Wow. That's *big* news, Bill. How'd that come about?" I didn't care about his response. Mentally, I'd stepped outside of the conversation to soothe myself with visions of moving our baby boys out of the tenement we called home and into something that didn't have paint chips peeling off the walls and cold air coming through the windows.

I knew we were on our way when, just days after he began at the Ford Motor Company, we got our very first credit card.

Such visions of hope became, only months later, delusions of grandeur. Billy Lesane, the man whom I had once seen as my best friend, with whom I had so much fun with and couldn't wait to marry, had transformed into a self-centered and detached man. I don't know if I just hadn't noticed this quality in him prior to this point—young love sometimes hides the bad qualities in one's mate—or if this selfishness had been lying dormant in him and decided to rear its ugly head once our marriage became routine. Regardless, I saw it in him now. He would spend almost his entire paycheck on himself, disregarding the fact that we had rent to pay, and food, formula, and diapers to buy. Along with this unveiling of his selfish behavior, he also started to show more of his domineering personality, something that grew worse with each pregnancy.

I don't believe that this behavior was a reflection of his love for his children—Bill welcomed each one of them with the same amount of love—but there was no denying the change in our relationship. I began to follow behind him, when I should have walked alongside him. I began to anticipate his desires and meet them before I acknowledged my own. His desires soon turned into "rules" and without protest, I acquiesced. The routine of taking care of my children and my husband drained every bit of energy from me. I had nothing left for myself and felt I was constantly walking on eggshells. I was taking care of four people but neglecting the most important one: me. The dream I had as a little girl of becoming a schoolteacher was slipping away from me, getting lost in the responsibilities I had at home. I tried to find happiness in the fact that I had a husband and a house full of children—something else that I'd dreamed of when I was very young—but despite the fact that this part of my dream had come true, I still wasn't happy.

It was challenging to live in a five-story walk-up with a barren and dismal back view of concrete and the fire escape. This didn't add much sunshine to the dark moods I'd begun to experience. Even to run to the corner store was an arduous task. My mother lived nearby and when she wasn't working, she would help out as much as she could. This was occasionally convenient for me, but with caring for three boys under the age of four, and hauling groceries and dirty laundry up sixty stairs in a shopping cart because there was no elevator, not much else in my life was convenient. Despite the obstacles that were presented to me during that time, I would tell myself over and over again, "Everything's gonna be okay, Jean. Everything's gonna be okay, Jean." It became my mantra.

Today, when I think about what it took to survive my own choices, I am incredulous. The choice to marry young. Very young. The choice to conceive not one child, but two, while I was still a teen. To have four more children all before I was twenty-five years old. These were decisions that designed my character, shaped my life, and lead me to the settled and complete feeling I now enjoy. But looking back, if I stood outside of my existence, I can barely grasp all that I took on.

And then … I became pregnant again.

CHAPTER TWO

And Then There Were Four

The only sentiment I could feel through my numbness was that I hoped it would be a girl. No, I didn't hope. I prayed.

After another easy pregnancy, my fourth child was born on October 10, 1967. We named him Gregory. Even though we'd been through it before, a new baby always brought the same celebratory emotions. Whispers that circulated throughout the family—things you'd expect family members to keep to themselves—were loud enough for me to hear. "Another boy? What are they gonna do with another mouth to feed?"

I defended myself and assured each and every one of them that I'd have one hundred boys, if that was what God saw fit for me, and I'd be just as satisfied. Secretly, though, I'd wanted a girl—not for the same reasons that most women want girls, but because I knew if we finally had a girl, Bill would've considered us "done."

My mother had moved into our small apartment by then because she'd lost her job and subsequently, her apartment. As you can imagine, our sleeping arrangements were getting rather cramped, and life in the Lesane family household on 158th in the South Bronx equaled chaos. There was my mother, our boys, my husband, who was now going off to the Ford Motor Company early every morning, and me, still trying to maintain a routine and my sanity to get through each day.

The morning we brought Greg home, I tucked him into our bed, and he slept right through the noise and commotion of the other children as they played throughout our small living space.

Bill worked from 7 a.m. until 3 p.m. Most of our conversations occurred during the dinner hour, between the endless "no's" and "don't do that's" we sprayed at the children as they sat at the dinner table, tied in their makeshift high chairs. We mostly spoke about his day at work or the boys. It was one of the few times during the day that Bill came into "our" world. It was almost as if he kept his independent world—the one, I thought, he was supposed to merge with his wife—as his first priority. The problem was, I gave up my own world and stayed in the one we created together.

One evening, during a dinner discussion about our children, Bill said something that truly exposed the level that his selfishness had reached. He alluded to feeling that having more children wouldn't be such a terrible thing. I knew, however, that if I had one more baby, I'd be stretched beyond my physical and emotional capabilities. I took a deep breath and made a mental note to call my obstetrician. It was time to get my tubes tied.

The very next day, I made the appointment to discuss the procedure. When I arrived at the doctor's office, I explained to him that I was done having children and that I believed getting the surgical procedure was my best option. He agreed and handed me a stack of forms.

"What is this?" I asked, my eyes skimming the words on the paper.

"If you'd like to move forward with such a procedure, you need to get the consent of your husband," the doctor informed me.

I felt as if I was a child, and the teacher had just handed me a permission slip for my parents to sign. I wanted to yell at the doctor,

"What the hell are you talking about? I don't have to get his permission each day when I have to gather up our children and usher them along to the bus to take care of my errands! I don't need a permission slip to maneuver our shopping cart down the five flights of stairs with all of *his* laundry in it and take it to and from the Laundromat each week. And I definitely don't need a permission slip when I have to prepare three meals a day, bathe each child, and tie each one of their little shoes!"

But I had to get permission to *not* have another child? Instead of yelling at the doctor, I did my best to give him a kind smile, took the forms, and sighed as I stared at the signature page.

When Bill returned home from work that evening, I became fearful. I knew he believed that getting my tubes tied was an unnatural process. I knew he'd say no. I feared the outcome so much that it was difficult to even get the words out, but still I had to ask.

"Could you please sign these papers?"

He read the papers, threw them on the table, and walked away. He left me standing there, with Greg, just weeks old, in my arms.

I retreated to my bedroom where I lay down and cried.

Bill's disregard for my decision, for my needs, and for my life was so overwhelming that I could feel my spirit die a little more that night.

~

By the time Greg was four months old, our routine was breakfast; playtime, while I washed the dishes and cleaned the apartment; lunch; walk to the Laundromat on laundry day; prepare dinner; eat dinner; bath and bedtime; tidy up the apartment once more before I went to sleep.

That was the general routine, unless I had to go to the market to buy groceries—that is, if there was any money left over from my welfare check. But the overall atmosphere in the apartment had finally settled.

And then came Daily.

Daily was the daughter of Diane, a friend of my younger sister, Afeni. She was a woman who wasn't fully equipped for motherhood at that point in her life. My sister asked me if I could take care of Daily "for a little while," and we welcomed the four-month-old into our family. I thought she'd be a nice playmate for Greg, as the two of them were only weeks apart in age. More important, I thought maybe she'd satisfy Bill's desire for a girl—he still talked of having a daughter, and I still hoped he'd change his mind about signing the paperwork for my tubal ligation.

The first night that we had Daily, I had to find a place for her to sleep. The three boys still shared one room, and Greg had already taken up the few extra inches in Bill's and my full-size bed. We had zero space, so I knew I had to get creative. I went from room to room, trying to find a comfortable but large enough space to put Daily down for the night and to store the few things her mother dropped off with her. I walked into our bedroom and stared at the large dresser. As Daily was only four months old, I knew she'd fit comfortably in one of the drawers on the bottom. So I filled it with a cushion and blankets, making it as comfortable as I could. She was sleeping through the night, so I knew this would be a good a place for her as long as she'd be with us.

Daily quickly integrated into our family routine, but the days turned into months, and Daily's mother didn't come for her daughter. While I couldn't imagine not wanting to see my child every minute—every second—of the day, I tried not to judge Diane. Instead, I spent my energy watching Daily and Greg develop alongside each other—they seemed very much the same. There were no distinguishable differences between the two babies' development at that time, although Greg was actually reaching a few milestones earlier than Daily. He sat up and fed himself before the age of six months. I attributed this to the fact that he had three older brothers, and he had to get his food when it was placed in front of him before they took it from him. During those months I even remember spending more time tending to Daily, because Greg was just easier, overall. He cried for my attention much less than Daily did.

Just as abruptly as Daily came into our lives, her mother came back, unannounced, and took her. Before I could even sort out my feelings about Daily's being gone, I discovered I was pregnant again—this was around Greg's first birthday. I wasn't excited, nor was I discouraged. I was numb. The only sentiment I could feel through my numbness was that I hoped it would be a girl. No, I didn't hope. I prayed.

For nine months, I prayed.

I was never so anxious to ask the doctor after a birth, "What is it?"

The doctor looked at me. "It's a gal."

That was it. I got the girl. And just like that, our family of six turned into a family of seven. My daughter, Jamala, was born on June 21, 1969.

My prayers had been answered.

CHAPTER THREE

My "Quiet" Child

I had always pushed aside any feelings that Greg was developing "differently" by telling myself that maybe he was just going to be my "quiet" child.

As Greg approached his second birthday, I was still waiting for him to say "Ma-ma" or "Da-da." And because my other boys had started forming two-word phrases much earlier than two years old, I started to wonder if there was a problem. Before that point, I had always pushed aside any feelings that Greg was developing "differently" by telling myself that maybe he was just going to be my "quiet" child.

Besides being "quiet," I also noticed that Greg didn't socialize with his brothers, his cousins, or the neighbor kids that would come over to play. He wouldn't sit down with his brothers while they played with their ABC blocks or their Hot Wheels cars. A rowdy game of cowboys and Indians, cap pistols and all, couldn't even capture his attention—until the cracking noise of the gun went off. Still, that wouldn't pique his curiosity and give him the desire to play; it would, instead, set him off in a negative way. He'd cover his ears as if the noise hurt him. Greg didn't like loud sounds. Even if it was something as simple as someone's talking louder than usual, he would cover his ears and rock back and forth. If his baby sister, Jamala, cried, he'd cover his eyes.

It was around this time that I realized that Greg didn't interact with anyone at all. Typically, he'd play alone all day long. While his older brothers played with the toys strewn throughout the apartment, Greg would pick one up, examine it, and then usually throw it over his shoulder and run off.

Now that the kids were older, I'd venture out of the house with them more often. Even a trip to the Laundromat was exciting for them. The kids would follow behind as I wheeled the shopping cart backwards down the flights of stairs. When we got to the sidewalk, they'd all hold hands with one another.

Our evening ritual was dinner, followed by bath time. I'd line up the kids, bathe them, and then sit them in a row to dry them off and lather them with baby lotion. Bill and Scott, the two oldest boys, were now old enough to warm the formula bottle for Jamala while I put Greg and Kenny in their nightclothes.

Billy, Scott, and Kenny often would take a break from playing to gently touch Jamala's cheek or try to make her smile. They'd try to bring her a bottle and shove it in her mouth or even tease her at times. But Greg was completely disinterested and unimpressed by her presence. Running through the house was more interesting to Greg than his new baby sister.

Our apartment included a long hallway that Greg loved. He would run from one end of the apartment to the other, as fast as he could. Then he would hit the wall at one end with his hands, turn around, and run the other way. He could do this for hours—back and forth, like a swimmer racing in an Olympic trial, hitting the wall to gain another lap.

And then there was that noise he'd make. "Ehhh!" he'd shriek. It was halfway between a scream and a grunt. He'd make it whenever he was excited, irritated, or needed my attention. It was the noise that would always cause Bill to say, "Could you hush him up, please?" or "Get him out of here, with all that noise."

Greg's second birthday came and went and still he hadn't said "Mama." As a matter of fact, he hadn't said anything. Not one word, not even babbling. Just "Ehhh!" Because Greg had no language, he pulled me around the house when he needed something—there was no way for him to communicate with me except to lead me to what he wanted. When he was thirsty, he would pull me by the hand into the kitchen and stand at the refrigerator, and I would then offer him milk or juice.

Now, the nagging feeling that something wasn't right with him grew into something that kept me up at night.

I started to analyze my children and their differences. And without fail, Greg always stood separate from my others. One interesting difference was that at age two, he had an intense interest in puzzles. He could sit all day long, putting together wooden puzzles, over and over again. We moved up to the 1000-piece puzzles by the time he was four years old. No matter how many hours it would take to finish—although he did get frustrated, sometimes even angry—he would sit there until he completed it.

To this day he has an affinity for puzzles—the kind of puzzles that require patience to do. Whether it was the wooden ones or the challenging ones made for adults, Greg could complete them with exceptional speed. I tried to engage my other children in the puzzles that Greg had mastered, but they showed limited interest and would move on to their toy trucks and homemade forts.

Another striking difference at that time between Greg and my other children was that he never included me in his play. The others would spontaneously show me a city of Legos that they'd built or the picture they'd colored. It was a natural thing for them to invite me into their world in this way. But not Greg. It was as if he existed in a separate world from the one in which the rest of the family lived.

When it was time to potty train Greg, I used the same method that worked successfully with my other kids. I started them all before their second birthdays and had them fully trained by the age of three. I had a set pattern that I thought was foolproof. But with Greg, his accidents never lessened. There was no success. No progress was made.

I started noticing other things about Greg that just seemed "different." For example, he would obsessively peel paint chips off the walls. If I'd let him, he would have done it for hours. But I would continuously shoo him away and firmly say, "Greg, no! No, Greg, go on out of here." Still, without fail, soon thereafter he'd be right back at the spot, picking off the paint chips and putting them in his mouth. Of all the things for him to play with in our apartment, I couldn't imagine why he focused on peeling the paint from the walls.

I voiced my concerns to Greg's pediatrician, but he brushed me off with empty excuses. He'd say, "Oh, Greg's development is delayed most likely because you have to spread your attention between all five of your kids," or "He may not feel the need to talk because he has older siblings." The doctor never found anything wrong with Greg. His body was healthy. In looking at him, nothing appeared out of the ordinary. He was a very handsome little boy. I didn't want to believe my gut feeling, which was telling me something wasn't right. Instead, it was easier to embrace the doctor's nonchalant response and allow it to ease my concerns.

CHAPTER FOUR

No Air Left to Breathe

I wanted so badly to tell her that I'd finally made the decision to leave Bill. I wanted to tell her that he had sucked all the air out of me. I wanted her to know that I had no plan, but that I just knew if he didn't leave, I would die.

Another tenement apartment at 1240 Woodcrest Avenue in the Bronx was the next place we called home. This time, we rented a unit that was on the ground floor. It had three bedrooms, one that we gave to my mother, who had recently lost her job again. Our personal space was indeed more crowded, but I was always thrilled to have my mother living with us. I thought maybe I would have more chances to actually venture out *without* the kids. Or perhaps I could even cultivate a friendship with my new neighbor, Mary Fraser, who lived above us.

During our occasional evening visits, Mary and I would sit on milk crates in front of the apartment and talk about our lives. I had this incredible urge to share my concerns about Greg with her, especially because she had four young children, but I was never brave enough to open up. So instead of sharing with her my shame and embarrassment, we'd laugh about things like how different our lives would be if we were wealthy, single, independent women with no kids. We'd also talk about our demanding husbands from time to time. This casual banter became my song and dance, a substitute for having to talk about and face the real issues in my life.

It became our therapy, too. On those evenings after dinner, she'd come to the door and ask Bill, "Can Jean come outside for a little bit?"

Although he didn't mind, I cringed at the fact that I needed his permission. It was as if a child was coming to the door to ask if her neighbor could come outside and play. I never spoke up and always waited for Bill to answer—I was simply too fearful of what the result might be if I did.

I'd make my way outside with a bottle of wine—it was our most common choice of beverage. Sometimes we'd get fancy and mix a pitcher of sangria.

On some nights, the ice cream truck would appear, and Mary's girls would run to her for money so they could buy an ice cream. My kids stopped asking me after they realized we didn't have any money for such treats.

Mary often talked openly about the problems that she and her drug-dealing husband were having. I was shy and never exposed too much about my husband, and when I did talk about Bill, it would be hesitantly—I'd practically whisper.

Still, I didn't talk about my concerns over Greg. I didn't even express my concerns about my little boy with my sister, Afeni, who was my closest confidant. Sometimes, though, during visits with her in her apartment, I'd break down and start crying.

"What's wrong? What's wrong?" she would ask.

Her boyfriend, Mutulu, would always be close by, and I felt self-conscious talking about my problems in front of him. Though I wanted to tell my sister that I knew in my gut that there was something wrong with Greg, no matter how many times the doctor told me everything was fine, I just couldn't. I was ashamed.

There were so many other parts of my life that needed fixing; there were so many things I wanted to change. I felt that if I laid out everything on the table for Afeni, she'd look at me differently than the big sister that I had always been to her. So I kept it all inside and only gave her my tears, without explanation.

Afeni had always been the one person I had shared everything in my life with, good and bad. I realized she needed to know what was going on with Bill, if nothing else. I couldn't deal with hating myself any longer and the private stress that was paralyzing me. I wanted so badly to tell her that I'd finally made the decision to leave Bill. I wanted to tell her that he had sucked all the air out of me. I wanted her to know that I had no plan, but that I just knew if he didn't leave, I would die.

CHAPTER FIVE

On My Own

*Greg's wandering across the street as he had was his way of telling me
that I could no longer deny the truth for one more second.*

I can still see so clearly the vision of my eldest child, Billy, watching
from the window as his daddy pulled away in the cab. It broke
my heart, but I couldn't deny the new freedom I felt. It was June 14,
1970, and it would be the last time I would see Bill for more than a
decade. I was twenty-three years old. No husband. Five children. In
a deep depression.

And then there was Greg.

I didn't have the luxury of wallowing in my bed all day, watching
television. I was simply too busy tending to my children and too
overwhelmed with my daily routine to continue trying to find
answers about Greg.

Soon after Bill left, something happened that made me realize
that I wasn't going to figure it out all on my own.

One morning I woke up and peeked into the boys' bedroom to
check on them, as I did every day. The three eldest were still asleep,
strewn throughout the room like ragdolls that were left out of
the toy box overnight. I counted one, two, and three: Billy, Scott,

Kenny ... but no Greg. He was not in the room at all. I went down the hallway and looked in the bathroom, the kitchen, and the living room. I stood motionless in the middle of the apartment, listening as hard as I could. Listening for his tiny footsteps. I waited for him to whiz by me on his way to nowhere. But he didn't. The only sounds I heard were the trucks rumbling by outside.

A different type of intuition, one that was more urgent, one that came with Greg's birth and was strengthening each day, made me run over to the window and look outside. There he was—*across the street!* I froze. He was dressed in nothing more than a diaper and was sitting on a crate in front of the bodega, staring into space and clapping. There was never a pattern to his clapping—it was just as sporadic as his rocking.

I hurried outside and across the street, then slowed my pace as I walked toward Greg, calling his name. When he looked at me, it was as if he looked *through* me. He would not keep his eyes on mine. He didn't care that his mommy was walking toward him or that he might be in trouble. He just sat there, observing his surroundings, until I reached him.

That was the moment I knew that there was something desperately wrong with my son. None of my children had ever wandered out of the house and across the busy boulevard. When I ran to Greg, he didn't look at me with the "Uh-oh! Mama is mad" expression that my other children often gave me. Greg didn't show one bit of remorse.

It wasn't long before whispers of possible mental retardation began to circulate in my family. The fact that Greg didn't *appear* to have mental issues, however, was misleading—and that's what kept me up at night. The thought that one of my children might not have the potential to live a full life made me feel vulnerable and scared. I was no longer going to let my pediatrician disregard my pleas for a medical justification. Greg's wandering across the street as he had was his way of telling me that I could no longer deny the truth for one more second.

CHAPTER SIX

The First Incident

*I had no point of reference for Greg's behavior. The mothers I knew
didn't have children who ran up and down hallways all day. Their kids
didn't rock back and forth; didn't wander out of their homes and cross the
street; certainly didn't pick chipped paint off the walls and eat it.*

While I was involved in my day-to-day activities, including
scolding my boys, changing diapers, carrying Jamala on my
hip, and making dinner for seven, my sister, Afeni, was in New York
City, heavily involved in the plight of the Black Panther Party. She
had no children yet, but her world seemed as frenzied as mine, although for entirely different reasons. We were both smack in the
middle of our adult lives; our innocence was waning and our sen-
sibilities were mostly formed. We had so much in front of us, but it
didn't matter because we were both living so hard in the moment.

Adding to our already heavy load was my sister's arrest in the
summer of 1969. She, along with twenty other Black Panthers,
were arrested for allegedly conspiring to blow up various American
landmarks. I'd watch news reports on my black-and-white television
that detailed my sister's trial. It eventually became the worldwide,
notorious Panther 21 trial. A flurry of supporters—some celebrity,
some not—raised enough bail for her to be released. Through it all,
Afeni became a celebrity herself.

This fame elevated her power in the community and at times, friends and family would ask me if I was envious of her. I admired her spirit, but wasn't envious of Afeni. It was more that I was afraid for her. We didn't necessarily agree with what the other was doing all the time, but in the moment, we couldn't always express that. As sisters, we always supported what the other was seeking to do. Afeni traveled and spoke with the Panthers to raise money. Her heart was in it. If I had confronted her about her activities, it would have been like tearing a piece of meat apart. She was my baby sister. She was a different soul. She was rebellious, the extreme opposite of me.

Afeni would bring everything she experienced in life back to my children and me. She exposed us to things we'd have never known about, things that to this day I am still grateful for. I was not envious of her; I was proud of her.

News reporters tracked down Afeni the moment she stepped out of jail. To prevent them from knowing where she lived, she would schedule media interviews at my apartment and at the apartments of her friends. A meeting at the residence of anyone with six children would be a challenge, but in my home there also was Greg. Even the sound of a loud conversations among guests in our home or the television volume turned too high would agitate him, so I knew I was taking a risk with regard to his comfort level to allow news reporters to enter the apartment.

I held my breath as the news crew entered our apartment, and I hoped that Greg could maintain his calm. We all watched as our common living space was transformed into the interview area. The lighting crew unfolded the equipment, and the reporters readied themselves, rehearsing their questions. All the while, I kept a mother's eye on Greg. Within the hour, my living room was packed beyond capacity. Besides the reporters and the camera crew, Afeni's associates who worked with her on the trial had come, in addition to a few of my friends.

After I walked down the hall to check on my sister, who was also preparing for the interview, I realized that the noise level in the house was growing rapidly. My small apartment, which was typically not a quiet zone, was now utter chaos. I tried to shush the children. But when I found myself unsuccessful in telling them to sit down and be quiet, I decided to shoo all of them, including Greg, down the hall and into their room. I couldn't, however, get Greg to follow with the rest of the children. That particular day, I did everything I could so that he didn't stand out. I didn't want any of the guests in my home to recognize that one of my children was "different." So I took a deep breath and continued to push them along. Greg wouldn't budge.

And then he started to make his noise. "Ehhh!"

I look around, praying that no one else had heard him. It was almost the same feeling as walking down the street and tripping, and then hoping that no one noticed—look around and keep on moving.

Back then, I had no point of reference for Greg's behavior. The mothers I knew didn't have children who ran up and down hallways all day. Their kids didn't rock back and forth; didn't wander out of their homes and cross the street; certainly didn't pick chipped paint off the walls and eat it. Their children were developing normally. I had so many people, so many family members around me, but I felt so alone. I was mute but wished I could scream to get someone to hear me. Yet the possibility of my fear being revealed overwhelmed me.

Greg did it again, louder this time. "Ehhh!"

One of the female reporters said to me, "Oh, he's so cute. Let him stay out here."

Immediately, I felt the embarrassment begin to rise within me. I continued to try to shush Greg, but he didn't care, simply because he didn't know what embarrassment was. He didn't know that the reporter was trying to engage him. He didn't care that Auntie Afeni was being interviewed about an important trial.

"How old are you?" the reporter asked Greg.

Before she could realize that Greg couldn't answer the question, I said, "He's two and a half."

"He's so cute," the reporter repeated.

"*Ehhh!*" Greg said, even louder than before. I should have told the reporter that this was Greg's way of telling her to leave him alone; that he was extremely annoyed. But that would've meant acknowledging what I'd worked so hard to hide: that Greg had special needs.

"Aw, you are so adorable," she cooed.

With that, my worst fears were realized, as Greg launched himself toward her—and bit her on her rear end. Hard.

The reporter yelped—loudly!

I was mortified, even though Greg's intentions weren't vicious. He simply wanted her out of his space. Before I could even take a breath and gather myself and apologize, the reporter withdrew from Greg and immersed herself into the crowd.

Because this was the first incident of Greg's to occur in front of people who were not members of our family, it was an important realization for me—and it was different from the one I had on the morning I found Greg across the street, sitting in front of the bodega. This time it was heavier, more pressing. Greg's unusual and unexpected behavior had been revealed to the outside world. I could no longer sweep his differences under the rug.

CHAPTER SEVEN

Finally, a Reason

I thought, 'Yes! Finally! Greg must be suffering from lead poisoning. That's why he can't talk!'

The biting incident wasn't the only sign that things were getting worse. Greg's wandering out of our apartment began to happen more often as the months went on. As kids get older, one of a mother's luxuries is not having to watch them every second of the day. But I quickly learned that this wasn't the case with Greg. I'd go into the boys' room and ask, "Where's Greg?" Sometimes they'd direct me to him; other times they'd look at me with an empty stare. If they were playing outside, Greg might wander off. If they were playing inside, he could find his way out of the apartment and down the street. There would be a frenzied search for him, during which we'd call his name over and over again, even though he would never respond.

Greg usually wandered off with no specific destination. When we eventually would find him, my heart rate would slow, I'd take his hand, and we'd all head back to the apartment.

One time, the police found him before we did, and they brought him home—Greg was sitting contentedly in the back of the police car. Greg's going missing became a familiar occurrence around our neighborhood. On some occasions, police command posts were set up, and the police would always ask the same questions of me: "What was Greg wearing?" and "What time was it when you last saw him in the house?" With each answer I'd make sure to tell them, "He doesn't talk. He can hear, but if you call his name, it's likely he won't respond." When the sun went down, they'd turn on a spotlight, and we'd sit there and wait nervously, patiently.

Greg's obsession with certain things, such as puzzles and running up and down the hallway, weren't harmful to his health, so for the most part, I would leave him alone when he was engaged in those particular behaviors. But I could not ignore the one obsession that possibly could have adversely affected his health—his obsession with picking the paint chips off the wall and putting them in his mouth.

It was always the same exchange. I'd say, "No, Greg, come on, leave that alone."

But Greg was in his own world. He couldn't understand what it meant when I told him no. He didn't understand that I was in charge. He remained in his world, alone. He seemed to wonder why I constantly told him that he couldn't do things, as if he didn't understand why he should have to listen to me.

By this time I had gotten a job. I began working as a tenant organizer with the Bronx Legal Services. We learned from larger organizers how to deal with issues that arose between tenants and landlords so we were better equipped to help members in our community. Some issues that were prevalent in tenement apartments in the ghettos of New York during this time were roach infestation, absentee landlords, no heat, and children being bitten by rats. We were able to help these tenants address their complaints and find some type of resolution. Even though my home life and my son's issues were a huge problem, these new responsibilities gave me a boost in my self-esteem that I hadn't felt in years.

One tenant/landlord issue in particular piqued my curiosity: the health risks of lead-based paint and the likelihood of its causing severe developmental delays in children. Slumlords tried to cut costs by painting fresh coats over old, which would result in layer upon layer of lead-based paint on the walls. Eventually, it would chip, peel, or sometimes even crumble into dust. Lead poisoning occurred when individuals ingested the harmful paint, allowing it to enter the bloodstream. The hazards of lead-based paint became a hot topic during the 1970s; news articles during that time often described the speech, language, and behavioral problems of children exposed to such paint. I thought this might be the answer to all my questions about Greg.

I decided to have my son tested. Sure enough, Greg's blood showed traces of lead.

It all made sense to me. I thought, *Yes! Finally! Greg must be suffering from lead poisoning. That's why he can't talk!*

I filed a lawsuit against the landlord who owned the building where we lived. In the end, I was awarded ten thousand dollars. In 1969, this was a substantial chunk of money. The court ordered that the money be placed in a bank account for Greg's needs. This changed everything for me. Not only did I have an answer to what was causing Greg's developmental delays, but it gave me hope that as the poison made its way out of Greg's system, he would get better. For the first time in his life, I felt a sense of relief. This meant that what many of us had suspected was, in fact, not true—it meant that my son was not mentally retarded.

CHAPTER EIGHT

A Breath of Fresh Air

I put on my Sunday best. I saw him as soon as I got to the restaurant. There he was, leaning up against the bar like John Wayne.

I thought finding the cause of Greg's developmental delay would lessen the shame for me, but I quickly found that it didn't. Among family and close friends, having a justification for Greg's "different" behaviors and speech problems decreased the embarrassment— now, at least, I had a concrete explanation—but I still lived with the anxiety of wondering how I would raise Greg if he didn't get better. How could I care for a child with special needs when I had my other children to raise as well?

With Bill gone, I felt myself blossoming into a new person; I felt good about myself outside of my being a mother. In addition to my new responsibilities at work, I began attending Lehman College. I became more involved with my community. I poured any energy that I had left over at the end of the day into the job and became the "go-to" person for tenant rights, and I organized events and information sessions for tenants to help them understand what their rights actually were. It was important for them to know that they were not accountable for their rent if the landlord did not meet his responsibilities; for example, if the tenants' trash wasn't picked up weekly. I'd travel by bus to different meetings, taking Greg along because asking someone to keep him was too large a favor. My friend Ernest Collier, however, was one person to whom I could go and not feel that I was asking too much. He worked on the People's Housing Coalition with me, and during meetings he would be the one to help me keep Greg happy. He would hold Greg's hand and keep him entertained and focused and, when needed, quiet. He could calm him down wonderfully if Greg got too excited or started to make noises.

On the nights when I didn't have to participate in a tenant strike, Mary and I would take a seat on our milk crates in front of the apartment building and watch our children play together. Between us, we had nine children, which gave us lots to gossip about. With Marvin Gaye songs playing in the background, the two of us would sit and mostly giggle about what our lives would be, once all our dreams came true. And behind our casual conversations, I'd secretly imagine my knight in shining armor, riding up to the front of the building and sweeping me off my tired feet, just long enough for me to catch my breath.

I should have been more aware of the old saying, "Be careful what you wish for." My knight did come, but he didn't ride up on a horse. He rode up in a New York City cab. I was sitting on the stoop with Mary when he pulled up. He jumped out and fixed his hat so that it was placed perfectly on his head, cocked to the side. He was dressed sharp—sharp enough to back that confident walk I couldn't miss as he approached us. I felt a surprising and immediate attraction.

Mary said to me, "Jean, this is my brother, Thomas Cox, but we call him T.C." He flashed me a smile that knocked the wind out of me as Mary continued, "T.C., this is Gloria Jean." If he spoke, I didn't hear anything. I was too caught up in the moment. Then Mary added, "Jean's married and has five kids."

I smiled on the outside, but my moment of thinking this was my new man was gone. I could've knocked Mary off her milk crate.

After hearing that, T.C. got what he came for from his sister and left quick. Real quick. I was sure that was the end of that.

To my surprise and delight, a few nights later, he returned. He took a seat with us in front of the apartment, flirting with me, drinking wine, bobbing his head along to Al Green's "You Ought to Be with Me."

I remember sitting in class at night, dreaming that Tom was waiting for me in his car at the bottom of the steps in front of the campus. Even though I thought it was too good to be true that we would actually ever be together, just hoping for it and anticipating it was like a breath of fresh of air.

Weeks later, as if I were in high school, I passed a note along to his sister and asked her to give it to him. The note read: "I want to have an affair with you."

I was so pleased with myself when he finally invited me out for dinner. I couldn't believe that I'd actually written a note so bold, and then I laughed because it worked! I hadn't laughed in a long, long time. It felt good.

"Where do you want to go?" he asked.

I didn't hesitate. "Wherever we can get chitterlings and champagne." Back then, that was the classiest dinner I could have dreamed of.

He didn't skip a beat. Our plans were finalized. We'd be meeting the next evening.

Tom was an employee for the Transit Authority. That was all it took to impress me, so I put on my Sunday best. I saw him as soon as I got to the restaurant. There he was, leaning up against the bar like John Wayne. I was star-struck, even though he wasn't a star! After a night of chitterlings, collard greens, candied yams, cornbread, and champagne, Tom and I started our love affair—a love affair that would last the rest of our lives.

Tom was the catalyst for my transformation into adulthood. Even though I was a mother of five, I had so much growing left to do when I met him. He forced me to grow up. He taught me to face myself. He encouraged me to tell the truth about life. He forced me acknowledge who I was and not run from it. He showed up at a time in my life when I was spreading myself so thin that I might have collapsed, emotionally, had he not come along.

CHAPTER NINE

A Brother Not Like Them

I would pick her up and look into her inquisitive eyes and say, "Yes Jamala, Greg knows you are his sister—his only sister. And if he could talk, he would tell you that he loves you very much."

When Greg was four years, my three eldest boys began to face the realities of having a brother who wasn't like them. They loved Greg; they just didn't fully understand him. I watched them try to explain these differences to their friends. As they passed Greg sprinting down the hallway, they would just say to their friends, "That's my brother Greg. He doesn't talk."

Their friends would quickly ask, "Why not?"

A common response from any one of my young sons would be, "Oh, because he eats the paint on the walls, and he got poisoned."

My two oldest, Billy and Scott, hid beneath a blanket of shame, much as I did; they made sure they stayed clear of Greg when they had friends over. Billy felt sorry for Greg. He'd fluctuate from being overbearing and protective to angry and saying he couldn't deal with it. It hurt him that there was nothing we could do to help Greg "get better."

My kids wondered why they had to shoulder such a heavy responsibility—the responsibility of having a disabled brother. I could see it all over their faces ... *Why me?* Even though we had a logical explanation for Greg's differences, my boys just didn't understand why Greg was the way he was.

Because the bulk of responsibility fell to Billy and Scott, simply because they were the eldest, it was easier for Kenny to embrace his little brother's differences. Or maybe because Kenny was my clown, my most mischievous boy, he dealt with Greg differently. He often made Greg his sidekick in various comedy acts. He would say to his friends, "Watch!" and he'd then say, "Greg, open your mouth." Greg would stand there with his mouth open in front of a small audience, not knowing or not caring why he'd been asked to do so. Then Kenny would take a glass of water and splash it at Greg's mouth for Greg to catch. Kenny seemed pleased with his brother, his cohort, and he laughed with his friends, who were amused but still a bit confused. Of course, Greg didn't laugh.

By the time Greg was four or five years old, I often would have his brothers take him along to the store with them. They were instructed to hold Greg's hand at all times so that he didn't wander off, and they always followed this instruction—they never "lost" Greg during one of these trips to the store. Greg didn't try to wander off because he couldn't wait to get to the store and have a sweets feast. Whenever they went to the store, Scott would gather milk and eggs and whatever grocery items I had written on the list. And Greg would grab all the cookies, candy, and doughnuts off the shelves. Scott would try to explain to Greg that he was not allowed to eat the food in the store, especially since he didn't have enough money to pay for it. But it was impossible for Greg to understand the concept of paying before he ate. Greg would start clapping, rocking back and forth, and grunting "Ehhh!" Thankfully, the storeowner understood that there was no reasoning with Greg, and each time they shopped in his store, he let Greg eat whatever he wanted without charging us for it.

Around the time that Greg was seven or eight years old, I asked Billy to take him to the basketball court on a regular basis. Part of me felt bad for giving this heavy responsibility to an eleven-year-old. Billy just wanted to enjoy a quick game of pick-up ball with his friends, but since Billy wanted to play every day, I thought that taking Greg along once in a while wasn't too much to ask.

Although Greg hurried along when told he was going to the corner market, it was a different story when I told him he was going to the basketball court with Billy. It was about a quarter of a mile from the apartment to the courts, and Billy often complained that Greg would stop and explore every sight in front of them as they walked down Jerome Avenue. Greg also would run into the street, unaware of the oncoming cars. I know it wasn't easy for Billy. He would grab Greg's hand and hold it tight as they crossed the street and headed toward the Mullaly Park basketball courts, which were across the street from Yankee Stadium. Once they got there, Billy would instruct Greg to sit down on a concrete slab on the side of the court and stay put. Most of the time he would just sit, rock, clap, stare ahead, or play in the dirt while waiting for his brother.

On one occasion, Billy noticed that his teammates were pointing and laughing at Greg. That's when Billy saw that his five-year-old brother had taken off his diaper and had peed in the dirt—something Greg often did, not caring where he was or who was watching. Now, he was playing in the mud—his dirt and urine concoction. Billy was extremely embarrassed; he marched off the court, snatched Greg out of the mud, and brought him home.

But even though they occasionally were embarrassed by Greg's behavior, all of Greg's brothers were protective of him, and they wouldn't stand for anyone teasing Greg. Billy and Scott were in many fights over the years in defense of their little brother.

The boys also would experience frustration when I relied on them to watch Greg when I had to run errands—they were usually so worried that something would happen to Greg while I was gone that it hindered their leisure time and fun. They had to keep a constant eye on him.

This frustration with Greg didn't stop there. I taught all my children to cook at a young age. I taught them to clean up and make their beds and to take out the trash. And it became expected for my two oldest, Billy and Scott, to make sure all chores were taken care of. All my children were making their beds every morning by the age of four—all except Greg. To teach him to make his bed was a daunting task; for that matter, it was daunting to teach him to do anything. He did not understand what it meant if I told him, "Pick up your toys." So Billy, Kenny, and Scott spent a lot of their time not only cleaning up after themselves but cleaning up after Greg as well.

The sibling relationship between my other children was typical—filled with love but sewn with rivalry. The relationship between Greg and his brothers, however, was much different. They loved Greg with all their hearts, but it was a different love than the one they shared with each other. It was different because of the fact that they weren't able to talk to him, and as children, this made them feel as though they didn't understand him. They gave him kisses and held his hand when we walked down the sidewalk, but Greg couldn't communicate with them, and they had to find other ways to understand his needs.

Biting was one way that Greg got his siblings' attention—he just needed a way to draw attention to himself. Unfortunately, as Greg got older, his bites became more painful. There was one time when all the boys slept together in the same room, and Greg bit Billy so hard, he nearly bit off his toe.

~

My younger children had a different experience with Greg. When Jamala turned five, her curiosity was met with confusion about her older brother. She would often ask me, "Why did God make Greg like this?" or "What do you think Greg would say if he could talk?" or "Does he know that I'm his little sister?"

I would pick her up and look into her inquisitive eyes and say, "Yes, Jamala, Greg knows you are his sister—his only sister. And if he could talk, he would tell you that he loves you very much." But the truth was that I really didn't know myself at this point if Greg knew who any of us were.

CHAPTER TEN

The Diagnosis

The doctor looked in my eyes and said, "Your son Greg has a neurological disorder. He is classified as autistic." That was the first time I had heard the word.

President Gerald Ford passed the Educational Amendments of 1974, the act that mandated that all academic institutions must accommodate special-needs children. And because Greg hadn't yet been to school, and there was no place for Greg in a mainstream academic environment, I believed that this would help me find a place for him. After the passing of the Amendments of 1974, social workers and guidance counselors were assigned to work with children with special needs. Today, if a child is diagnosed with autism, for example, a team of professionals who are trained to work with autistic children may be called in, and parents will enroll their child in the appropriate programs. But in 1974, there were no centers in our area that specialized in autism.

Over the years, I had voiced my concerns about Greg with his pediatrician, but I got nowhere with that—he always insisted that Greg was fine. Finally, however, after a referral from my sister's friends, the Kagans, I went to New York's Albert Einstein School of Medicine to have Greg evaluated. They did a series of tests on him, and I went back a few weeks later to get the results of the evaluation.

The doctor looked me in my eyes and said, "Your son Greg has a neurological disorder. He is classified as autistic."

That was the first time I had heard the word.

I sat completely still, trying to absorb what the doctor had just revealed to me. I tried to make sense of the diagnosis and of the word he'd just thrown at me. The year was 1975, and autism wasn't a commonly diagnosed disorder; in fact, it was considered "rare"— only one in 10,000 children was diagnosed as having autism at that time; today, it's one in 150 children.

The fog in my mind began clearing a bit. I don't quite know why, but having an "autistic" son *sounded* like it would be easier than having a son who was mentally retarded.

After learning of Greg's diagnosis, I began to research the specifics, and it all finally made sense. I learned that the speech of children who suffer from autism is often absent or delayed. Their social capabilities are severely limited or completely absent. I learned that a common trait of some children and adults with autism is that they don't understand emotion—they don't display sympathy for others; they don't offer hugs and kisses. Greg never hugged me, kissed me, or cuddled with me, as my other children did. If one of his brothers cried, or if his baby sister, Jamala, cried, Greg never had a reaction—other than to cover his ears and run away if the cries were loud enough.

~

The following two years were filled with joy and happiness but also with fear and trepidation. The fear was that my mother, who had suffered a stroke in August of the same year, would not make a full recovery; the joy was from my and Tom's decision to finally get married after being together for more than five years. And the happiness was from the birth of our son, Katari, on December 30, 1976. He was my sixth child and Tom's fifth child, but he was our only son together.

The difference between having Bill as my husband and having Tom as my husband was night and day. With Bill, I had to go on welfare, even while he was working at Ford Motor Company. He did not share his money with me or the children and the household in any way whatsoever. Tom, on the other hand, took care of everything. He took care of me and *all* of my children. He provided for us unselfishly. He was a kind man.

We'd moved into a three-bedroom apartment, one that was a bit nicer than any of those we'd lived in previously. Jamala shared a room with Tom's daughter, Me-Ling, and the boys shared the other. Our new baby, Katari, slept in our bedroom. Even with all the kids and the confined living space, we felt like we were moving up in the world.

CHAPTER ELEVEN

Summer on Coney Island

Greg just walked into the community swimming pool one summer and figured it out how to swim. It was one of the oddest, most remarkable things I'd seen.

There were times when I would leave Greg with my family or friends so I could run errands or go to work. One time I left him with Louisa, a long-time friend who had no knowledge of autism; she just thought Greg was quirky. I would often bring him to Louisa's to play with her son, Shane, who was a few years older. The two would run around outside together—Shane would say, "Come on, Greg!" And the two would take off. At first, Louisa felt comfortable with this, but when I alerted her that Greg would sometimes wander out of our home, she became more cautious and eventually didn't allow the two to be outside alone. Instead, she would create activities for the boys inside her house.

Louisa discovered that one of Greg's favorite things to do was to cut perfect shapes from butter. He would use Louisa's welfare butter that came in big square blocks as if it were clay, and he would cut it into stars, circles, crescent moons. She was amazed; here was this child who had been diagnosed with a rare disorder, but he could create things that her children, who were considered normal, could not. Louisa would report that Greg could draw exceptionally well, too. She would give Greg a few pens, pencils, and paper and maybe some crayons. He'd sit at the table, calm, in the middle of her rowdy household, and draw quietly for several hours. His drawings were beautiful. And just like his butter, they were always symmetrical.

One year, Louisa kept Greg for an entire summer. I asked her to take him so that he'd have some consistency in his life, something he wasn't getting at his own home because both Tom and I were working and had all of my other children to tend to.

At Louisa's home in Coney Island—just one block from the shore of the Atlantic Ocean—Greg got that daily routine that he needed. Louisa's brother Nelson, who was living with her at the time, took Greg and Shane down to the boardwalk every morning, where they walked the entire length of it. Greg especially loved it. After they returned from their morning walk, they'd have lunch, take a nap, and relax during the later afternoon until dinner was ready. This routine that Louisa provided for Greg was exactly what he needed, and I knew that I couldn't give it to him myself.

~

When Greg returned at the end of summer, life back at home with all his siblings was much different. There wasn't much time for me to tailor my treatment toward Greg, and Tom didn't either. He always treated Greg the same as treated everyone else. He'd often say, "Leave that boy alone. He'll talk when he's ready." Because our younger kids saw that we didn't necessarily treat Greg differently, they treated him the same as well—even though Jamala continued to be confused by his behavior. She once asked me, "Mama, why do I have to ask Greg to pass the plate a million times before he responds?"

As Greg got older, we had to watch him more carefully with his food choices. It seemed that he could never get his food spicy enough. We would catch him as he tried to pour the whole bottle of hot sauce on one piece of chicken. Greg's siblings did try to help curb his use of hot sauce, but I could tell they were afraid he might stab them with his fork if they tried to take away the hot sauce.

We also had to make sure that he didn't hurt himself as he got more reckless in his behavior. I'd often walk into the bedroom and find him jumping off the top of the bunk beds, doing somersaults and flips from one bunk bed to the other. And when the kids would go to the pool, Greg would do wild flips into a crowded swimming pool. He had no regard for anyone who might be in his path.

Greg was a natural, instinctual swimmer. I never had to enroll him in swimming lessons as I did with my other children. Greg just walked into the community swimming pool one summer and figured out how to swim. It was one of the oddest, most remarkable things I'd seen with respect to his behavior. And he had the same uncanny ability to jump off of high places and land on his feet. He was very catlike. Tom and I would take our children to Central Park on the weekends so that they could kick a ball around or so we could have a picnic. And it never failed that Greg would find the highest rock, climb it, and then, with reckless abandon, jump!

The older Greg got, the greater the dangers became—both to him and other people. When he bit, he bit harder. When he threw himself into in the pool, it was like a hundred-pound bomb.

Finally, the reality that we needed to place Greg in special care became too strong to ignore.

CHAPTER TWELVE

Cheshire, Connecticut

He didn't cry. He didn't yell out, "Mama! Don't go!" and throw a tantrum on the floor. He was oblivious to whether I was there or I was gone.

The realization of knowing I had to place Greg in a facility was the hardest part of my journey with him. This transformation of consciousness—this knowing, this certainty that I could no longer raise Greg along with my other children in a three-bedroom apartment—was more obvious with each new year. I found a place in Cheshire, Connecticut, that had an opening. It was a home that housed children with special needs, mostly with physical disabilities. I knew if Greg received twenty-four-hour help from trained professionals, he would be safe. And so would his siblings.

Louisa rode along with me on the long drive to Connecticut when I first took Greg. Greg sat in the backseat and stared out of the window while Louisa and I shared a few hours of conversation—small talk to shade the complex emotions I was feeling at that time. Every few miles or so, I glanced through my rearview mirror and made promises to Greg. I said, "Greg, they are going to take such good care of you at this new place I found for you."

I knew that Greg would be much safer in an environment where he couldn't just wander off, where he'd be watched at all times, and his behavior—including his propensity for biting—would be monitored, I hoped he might even be taught to communicate and to use the bathroom appropriately so he could get rid of the diapers he still was wearing at nine years old. I knew it was the right decision, but I also knew it would be hard to leave my son, hard to accept that I would not see him that night before he went to bed.

Louisa tried to comfort me. "It's the natural process of things. You're doing the best thing for him."

As we entered the small town of Cheshire, I was immediately taken by the beauty of the town. Coming from an urban city built on concrete, I was in awe of the trees and the golden-brown shades of the autumn leaves.

The facility was a large country home, and it was spectacular. When we stepped out of the car, I inhaled the fresh, crisp air and marveled that it felt so different than what we were breathing in the Bronx. My sadness had slowly turned to feelings of relief. I gazed at the building and the grounds—how warm and inviting it all was—and my decision to place Greg here didn't seem such a bad one after all.

After we got Greg settled in, I toured the grounds with the coordinator. I saw a few kids who were severely handicapped, both physically and mentally. Many of them were wearing football helmets. I tried not to stare, but it occurred to me that they didn't look like Greg. Their handicaps were more obvious. I wondered if Greg would be made to wear a helmet. As the coordinator talked about the program, I learned that the facility didn't rely on medication for behavior modification, I again became reassured with my decision.

When Greg was settled in as much as he could be on the first day of a new environment, Louisa and I left. He didn't cry. He didn't yell out, "Mama! Don't go!" and throw a tantrum on the floor. He was oblivious to whether I was there or I was gone.

Later that evening, as I walked through the door of my apartment without Greg, the realization that he was not with me was suddenly unbearable. But I knew I'd lifted a heavy load from his siblings' shoulders, and this brought a sense of true peace to my otherwise broken heart. There was no more, "No, Greg," or "Where's Greg?" or "Greg, stop!" My other children finally had the freedom to have fun.

~

It had been difficult to care for Greg when I had to care for the other children, too, but that hadn't been the only problem we'd faced. Tom and I lost our apartment, which made me even more grateful I had found the facility in Cheshire for Greg. Louisa graciously invited us to move in with her—something that likely would not have happened if Greg had still been with us.

The two-hour journey from New York to the small town in Connecticut was a beautiful drive. Most of the time, Louisa would travel with me. Once, just after we crossed the Tappan Zee Bridge on the New York State highway, we were hit with thick, thick fog. The visibility was zero—the car in front of me was using hazard lights, but I still could barely see it, and I prayed out loud that I wouldn't hit anything. Driving through the fog and not knowing what was two feet in front of me was just how my life was going at that moment.

With each visit to Cheshire, I would be reminded that Greg didn't really care whether or not I was there. He knew I was his mama, but I didn't feel that he had any interest in my visits. He never showed excitement when he saw me, although I realized that he didn't have the capability to convey his emotion, his love.

I still had some of the money from the lead paint lawsuit, which I used to buy Greg's seasonal wardrobe each year—a new winter coat each September and T-shirts and light pants in the spring. I also would bring him small gifts that I thought he'd appreciate. Most of the time when I visited, Greg and I would sit together or walk the grounds. I saw progression in his communication skills with each visit. It was slow and gradual, but I was amazed.

He entered the facility when he was nine years old and still wearing a diaper. Within the first year at Cheshire, Greg was completely out of diapers.

There were a few times when I visited that he was wearing a football helmet. I was surprised and saddened by this—the helmets were for the kids with physical disabilities. I soon learned, however, that the helmet was for Greg's protection. If he was wearing a helmet, it meant that Greg had recently had an "incident" or had been rocking back and forth excessively, to the point where his case workers believed he needed to wear the helmet to prevent head injuries.

Overall, however, I felt very comfortable with Greg's new situation. He was living in a home that facilitated his needs in every way. It was a completely different way of life for him. He'd gone from a tenement-style apartment in New York to a plush facility among the trees in Connecticut—a place that was a lush green in the summer and snow-covered in the winter. He also was in an environment where most of the kids were white—a world completely opposite from the one where he'd spent his first nine years.

At Cheshire, Greg learned to communicate his basic needs. When Greg lived at home, he would bite and pull people around the house to get what he wanted; now, he used a clear, concise form of communication. He learned sign language and eventually learned to write. After Greg came back from Cheshire he would write words such as "Oreo cookies," "peanut butter," "jelly," and "chocolate." His penmanship was extremely neat and very precise. His handwriting was better than any of my other kids—better even than my own.

With each of Greg's new accomplishments, my decision to place him at Cheshire was reaffirmed. He'd grown tremendously in such a short time.

CHAPTER THIRTEEN

Back from Cheshire

I would see the kids try to teach Greg how to talk. Scott would take him into a room and try really hard to teach him how to say words. Greg would get so frustrated. Scott would say over and over again, "Come on, Greg, you can talk!" I wasn't sure that Greg would ever say a word, but I recognized the hope that Greg's new accomplishment brought to our family.

At the age of twelve, Greg "aged out" of Cheshire, and I could find no other facilities that would take him. As much as I wanted him to continue his growth in an environment like Cheshire, I had to bring him back home.

I thought that the best thing I could do for him was to make space in the house so that he was able to have his own room. It was a very small room, but I knew that it would be easier for him to adjust back into the family if he had his own living space. The apartment we lived in on 7th Avenue in New York was a five-floor walk-up, a small three-bedroom. Afeni had an apartment in the same building. Her children—Sekyiwa, who was four years old, and Tupac, who was eight years old—spent a lot of time at my apartment while Afeni was at work.

Even though our quarters were once again cramped, we made it work. Greg got right back into the routine of our family.

By the time Greg rejoined the family, Billy and Scott had moved into their own apartments. Kenny was gone, too—he had enlisted in the U.S. Navy. We all enjoyed Greg much more, now that he'd learned to communicate. He was still a lot to handle, but we all experimented with teaching him certain skills because we had seen so many improvements after he returned from Cheshire. I would see the kids try to teach Greg how to talk. Scott would take him into a room and try really hard to teach him how to say words. Greg would get so frustrated. Scott would say over and over again, "Come on, Greg, you can talk!" I wasn't sure that Greg would ever say a word, but I recognized the hope that Greg's new accomplishment brought to our family.

He was able to use sign language, and we picked up on the fundamentals and began to use it as well. He also learned how to write his name and a few of his favorite words, which were mostly food items that he wanted. My youngest son, Katari, was just a baby when Greg first came home from Cheshire, but he remembers the admiration he held for him in the following years, when he realized that he had an older brother who was not quite like his other brothers. Katari used to tell me that he thought it was *cool* that he had a brother who had autism. It was interesting to see the differences between his older siblings who felt a huge responsibility to Greg versus his younger siblings who looked up to him as an older brother.

Greg had also begun to figure out new ways to ask for things that he wanted, such as through picture collages. He'd flip through magazines and find the foods he liked. He'd cut out pictures of Oreos, Cap'n Crunch cereal, and pictures of spaghetti and chicken.

My house was filled with other children in addition to my own. My niece and nephew, Sekyiwa and Tupac, often stayed at my house when their mom worked. And Louisa's kids, Shane and Malcolm, were over quite often. Greg used to write down what he wanted—like "bean pie"—and give the note to the children so they could get things for him. (Katari used to ask me all the time, "Ma, how come he can write but can't talk?" I'd admit that I was confused by that as well.) Bean pies were one of Greg's favorites. He would write "bean pie" on a piece of paper and give it to Tupac. And it would never fail that Tupac would get Greg a bean pie, even if he had to leave the house and hunt one down on the street.

Despite the fact that Greg had made great progress, there were some old ways that remained. He hadn't lost his habit of biting. One night, my husband and my sister and I were sitting on the couch, watching television. We had successfully put all the kids to bed at a reasonable hour—all except for Greg. Afeni said, "Okay, Greg, it's time for you to go to bed." Greg ignored her. So Afeni said again, "Okay, Greg, it's time for you to go to bed now." Greg turned around and bit her. He clamped down on her leg and would not let go. Tom had to actually punch Greg to get him to stop biting Afeni. I was mortified as I watched, Tom, a man who loved Greg as if he were his very own son, hit him with all his force, so that he'd stop biting Afeni. I felt shame. I felt sick. I wanted to scream.

The next day I scheduled a meeting with a social worker. I asked that she help us find another school or facility for Greg, a place for him to receive instruction and care. On the day of the scheduled meeting, I was apprehensive. The meeting was to take place in our apartment, and a home visit was not my preference. I was living in real ghetto apartment inside a five-floor walk-up. To have others come into this place was not ideal. I heard the knock at the door and on my way to answer, I stopped at the kitchen to check on Greg. What I saw made me gasp. Greg had taken the peanut butter and jelly out of the refrigerator and spread it on the walls and on the table. It was everywhere. I shook my head and sighed. Then I thought to myself, *Maybe if the social worker sees this, she'll help me find a program for him.* So I held my breath and opened the door.

Unfortunately, it made no difference. It was two years before we found another facility for Greg.

CHAPTER FOURTEEN

Bronx Mental Hospital

It was as if a loud voice was thundering over me, "GREG DOESN'T HAVE A CLUE!" He was just disconnected from me completely. … That day I had one of the most significant moments of clarity I'd had throughout my entire journey with Greg. He didn't know what "mama" meant.

Greg spent the latter part of his teenage years with me, as Tom and I shuttled our family from one apartment to the next, trying to keep the rent paid and food on the table, all while trying to maintain a peaceful environment for Greg so that the number of incidents were minimal. But caring for Greg was an arduous task. Day in and day out, he had to be watched, tended to, and taken care of in every way. I had to help him bathe, get dressed in the morning, watch everything he ate, and make sure he didn't wander out of the house. I had to give Greg as much attention when he was seventeen years old as when he was three years old, if not more. I didn't mind that it took extra time to take care of my child. It was just that all of the time I had to give him limited what I was able to do for the other kids. No matter what I did, someone was being neglected. I didn't have enough eyes, hands, or hours to take care of all of them.

I had Greg evaluated every few months by various social workers and school district employees. They'd give me hope of finding a place for Greg, but it never worked out. They'd tell me there would possibly be an opportunity for Greg in New Hampshire. Then they'd tell me about something possibly coming up in Pennsylvania. Months turned to years and still nothing panned out. Nothing.

One summer, I took Greg to yet another evaluation. We rode the bus across town, ten blocks or so. The social worker presented Greg with a series of tests, most of which Greg had taken previously. He was going through them easily and quickly. But after a couple hours passed, Greg began to tire. He started to resist and let out a few "Ehhhs," but the social worker continued to put more tests in front of him. I wanted Greg to at least finish because my hopes were now higher than ever for finding a placement for him. I was trying to hide the fact that he was tired because I wanted her to see how advanced and high-functioning he was.

I said to him, "Come on, Greg, one more time. You can do it!" I knew if the social worker could see all that I saw, we could get him into the next level for placement. But I realized about thirty seconds later that I was in denial.

"Ehhh!"

"Come on, Greg. You can do one more."

Of course I knew what *Ehhh* meant. I knew that I should've said to the woman who was administering the tests that it was time to leave because he was tired. He was done. But I didn't. I just continued to urge him.

And then it happened. He stuck me with a pencil!

I never thought he'd lash out at me. He had attacked his brothers, my sister, and strangers, but I was sure he'd never hurt me. My emotions collided in that one moment. I was mad. I was sad. I felt hopeless. I couldn't hide any of what I was feeling any longer. I grabbed him by the hand and snatched him out of his seat. As we walked to the front entrance, I dropped his hand and walked in front of him. I was angry and ashamed at the same time. Why did I have to go through this? Why did I have to figure this out? I felt so alone.

"Come on!" I yelled to the space behind me, not even turning my head. I knew Greg hadn't been trying to hurt me. He was just tired. I knew it was my fault. But my frustrations sometimes boiled over when I felt hopeless and fearful of his future, especially when I couldn't get him to put in the effort to ensure a good placement.

Calming down a bit, I finally grabbed his hand again as we approached Central Park West. I was still walking fast, though, and was practically dragging my twenty-year-old son behind me. And then I stumbled on a crack in the sidewalk and fell flat on the ground. Even though I was just over forty years old, I felt like an eighty-year-old. The years had caught up with me, physically and emotionally. I felt exhaustion in every one of my bones in that very moment.

Greg just stood there. I stared up at him, waiting for him to help me up. He didn't reach down to give his mother a hand. He just stood there and clapped, making his happy sounds—"Eeow! Eeow!" Then he started dancing. And then rocking.

I got up and brushed the dirt off my pants. I tried to brush the bad mood away, but it wasn't going. I just kept replaying the last minutes in my head, from the pencil moment to my falling on the sidewalk. And during this replay, I finally got it. It was as if a loud voice was thundering over me, "GREG DOESN'T HAVE A CLUE!" He was just disconnected from me completely. He did not understand that he was supposed to help me. That day I had one of the most significant moments of clarity I'd had throughout my entire journey with Greg. He didn't know what "mama" meant.

~

Finally, one of the social workers called to say that there was an opening at the Bronx State Mental Hospital. Just the sound of it scared me. I never wanted to send Greg to a mental hospital—he wasn't classified as "mental," so I was leery. I went in for the interview and tour and saw that there was a floor for young people who didn't fit into the "mentally disabled" category. On the floor where Greg would live, most of the others had physical disabilities, such as muscular dystrophy or cerebral palsy. Greg was the only one out of thirty to forty patients who had been diagnosed with autism. It was still hard for me to accept the fact that Greg needed twenty-four-hour care, just as these children did. But I realized that this was his only option, so I decided to give it a try.

On one of my visits, I noticed that Greg had a tooth missing. My heart sank as the social worker told me that Greg had had an incident with one of the male aides. Greg had bitten one of them, and the aide had punched Greg in the mouth so he would release his bite.

As a consequence, they told me that they put him on a drug called Thorazine. That was the last thing I wanted to hear. They told me that they typically used two different drugs to stabilize the mood swings and to curb outbursts. I didn't care what their policies were. The one thing I did know was that I did not want Greg on Thorazine. Thorazine was the same drug that was used for schizophrenic patients. I didn't want him to become a zombie. The alternative offered was Haldol, and I was more comfortable with that; I didn't want Greg to bite anyone else. And I certainly didn't want anyone else to have to punch my son in the mouth so hard that he would lose another tooth. Even though I was adamantly against using drugs for behavior modification, I allowed it now, for a few months, until I found another place for Greg. By the end of the year, I went to get Greg to bring him home.

CHAPTER FIFTEEN

A Home for Greg

Those phone calls were my lifeline. It was almost as if the phone calls let me know that I was not a terrible mother, not someone who had deserted her son.

I was so enthusiastic when I heard about the Institute of Applied Human Dynamics. Once again, I had hope for Greg's future. In 1991, when Greg was twenty-two years old, I enrolled him in this residential program that is designed to assist special-needs children and adults with fundamental life lessons so that they are able to live independently. Greg was trained in their day habilitation program, as well as vocationally. Each day he was taken to a place where he learned how to assemble ballpoint pens. After his day was over, he rode the van back to the group home—he was a resident at the Nereid facility. Nereid was a twenty-four-hour-a-day residential habilitation center. He lived with eight to ten other adults, all of whom had special needs.

Life for Greg at Nereid was as comfortable as it was for him in Cheshire, Connecticut. I was relieved that he was in a "home" versus a mental hospital. Even when they told me that he'd had a few incidents the first year and that they were going to prescribe Zoloft for him, I was satisfied with their decision. During my visits to see

Greg, he seemed at peace. It was as if he'd found a place where he was content. I knew he'd be here for quite a while. The wonderful thing about Nereid was that he couldn't age out, as he had at Cheshire. And he wouldn't be given anything stronger than an anti-depressant—no Haldol or Thorazine, as they did at the Bronx State Mental Hospital.

Tom and I decided to move south to Atlanta, Georgia. Our kids were all adults now, off doing their own thing, and Tom and I wanted to relocate where my sister and her children, Sekyiwa and Tupac, had already moved. When I made the decision to move, I was faced with the dilemma of what to do with Greg. Should I find a place in Atlanta and uproot him? Or should I keep him where he seemed happy and where I knew he was well cared for? As I went back and forth inside my head about it, I kept returning to the fact that I'd be disrupting Greg by taking him out of an environment to which he'd grown accustomed. The thought of removing him from the place where he seemed content was heartbreaking. I couldn't do it.

I decided that I would still just have to maintain my visits to see him, no matter how far he was from me. I remember during one visit in the year 2000, I met Doris, another resident of the Nereid group home. She was just a kid, much younger than Greg. Her family had deserted her and never came back to visit after they'd dropped her off. Meeting Doris and learning about her background caused me to feel guilt. Part of me felt that I'd deserted Greg when I moved. I didn't know how to process these feelings.

In the months afterward, I would call Greg's social worker, Ms. Robin Coleman, and check in as often as was appropriate. It helped me tame the guilty feelings that ran rampant inside my heart. During one of our conversations, I asked her opinion on transferring Greg to Atlanta. She said to me, "No, I don't believe you should. Greg is happy here. He really is. He has a routine. And you don't know how he'll react to a new environment or facility down there. It's best to leave him here." With that, I was able to release a bit of the guilt. But still it nagged at me more often than not.

I continued my calls to Ms. Coleman every few weeks and received evaluations every three months. I called so often that eventually our conversations didn't have room for anything other than my asking, "How's Greg?"

And she'd respond, "Greg's doing fine."

"Does he need anything?"

"No, he's doing just fine."

That became the extent of our conversation. Nothing much could be said after that because nothing much had changed from day to day with Greg. Those phone calls were my lifeline. It was almost as if the phone calls let me know that I was not a terrible mother, not someone who had deserted her son.

On the times that I traveled from Atlanta to New York to see Greg, I would see Ms. Coleman in her office. It was important to me that she knew I wasn't a "bad" mother. Then I'd travel over to the Nereid home to see Greg. My visits with him typically didn't last more than twenty minutes or so.

One weekend, I drove up to New York for a visit and when I got to the New Jersey Turnpike, I called ahead to let them know I was almost there.

They connected me to the social worker inside the house. "Greg's not here," she said.

"Where is he? I'm about thirty minutes away."

"He's in Atlantic City. Ms. Williams took him with her to the Clarion to gamble," the social worker said. She explained that Greg had earned money in the house doing chores and that he liked to gamble. This was the best news I'd heard in a long time. Greg had hobbies and desires. Greg could enjoy himself. He liked to gamble!

When I arrived at the home, Greg still wasn't back. Apparently, Greg was fortunate enough to be selected to go on that trip because he was considered "high functioning." I was eager to see my son, though, so I ended up waiting inside my car so I could greet the van when it pulled up. Finally, the van pulled in, and Greg got out with his bucket of change.

I jumped out of the car, calling, "Hey, Greg!"

He walked right past me and into the house. I followed him, but he walked straight upstairs. Minutes later, he returned, wearing his pajamas and his robe. He sat with me for a moment, and I talked to him and rubbed his head and touched his face. But the impression he gave me was that I was intruding; that he was happy where he was. I sensed that he hoped I wasn't trying to take him with me.

Selfishly, I was sad, but overall, I was happy he seemed so satisfied with his surroundings, with his life. He'd been going on road trips and gambling in Atlantic City. He seemed to be doing just fine.

The next morning I came back so we could spend more time together. Still, I didn't know where we were going to go or what we were going to do, and I felt a bit awkward because I hadn't been with Greg in public for a while. I didn't know what to expect.

Greg got in the backseat. I should have just said, "Greg, ride up here with me." But I didn't. I decided to let him do whatever it was that he was accustomed to doing. I took him to the House of Pancakes for breakfast. He wrote down a piece of paper: pancakes, bacon, eggs, milk. He picked up his utensils before the meal came and just waited.

I was shocked at how fast Greg ate his meal. I told him, "Greg, don't eat so fast." But before I could get the entire sentence out of my mouth, he was almost done with every morsel of food on his plate. I sat there, dumbfounded. I'd never seen anyone eat a plate of food this quickly.

After our breakfast we drove around New York. I talked to him about the sights. I pointed things out to him that were familiar, but he wasn't interested in any of it. And sadly, it didn't even seem he was interested in me. I realized that I was riding around the streets of New York with Greg in the backseat of my car—and that I was doing it for me, not for Greg. He wanted to be at the group home, back in his routine, not driving around aimlessly with me. I took him back and walked him inside to say good-bye.

~

A year passed before I traveled to New York to see him again. This time I took my granddaughter, Imani, and my great-niece, Nzingha. I was a bit afraid of what I'd see when I walked in this time because Ms. Coleman had retired and was no longer my contact. I was still able to call the facility to make sure Greg was okay, but it was just different now because they didn't seem to be as organized since Ms. Coleman had left. I wasn't receiving the evaluations as often. I felt more like a stranger during this visit.

When I walked in, I immediately saw Greg. He was busy setting the table. The atmosphere was peaceful, and Greg looked content. After that visit, I cried when I left. My granddaughter looked up at me and asked me, "Why are you crying, Grandma?"

"Because I'm happy. I'm happy that Greg is okay."

CHAPTER SIXTEEN

My Angel

My family and I think Arnetta is a phenomenal person—she has treated Greg like a member of her own family. We are amazed and appreciative that she took on this kind of responsibility and shared such love for somebody else's child. I consider this amazing woman my eldest daughter. I call her my darling and my angel sent from God. It was preordained that we should meet.

In 2001, a woman named Arnetta Marie Kinsley walked into the Nereid facility, and my life was never again to be the same. She'd come from a life of poverty and hardship. She had been cleaning houses to make ends meet and didn't have enough money for assistance for her own daughter, who was also a special-needs child. When she accepted employment as an aide at Nereid, Arnetta had no idea what she was getting into. She hadn't finished high school, so it was difficult for her to make all the pieces of life's puzzle fit together. Nereid hired her because of the invaluable experience she gained raising her own special-needs child. At first, she was the part-time recreation aide. Her job was to create activities for Greg and the other residents to keep them busy. She told me that Greg would always want to draw. He'd pick his favorite colors out of the big bin of crayons and fill in his shapes.

Over the course of the first year, Greg and Arnetta developed a special connection. Maybe because he was one of the highest functioning adults there, it was easier for Arnetta to communicate with him. I believe it was then that they began to speak their own special language. Arnetta learned what made Greg happy. She knew his likes and dislikes—so much, in fact, that Greg began to only go to her for what he needed. As time went on, she began to notice that he'd hum his little songs more often than he'd make his "Ehhh" sounds. She would later share with me that these "happy sounds" were an indicator for her to know he was all right.

In Nereid, Greg began using a pad of paper to communicate what he wanted to eat. Most of the time, it was pancakes—he'd write "chocolate" or "strawberry." Another way Arnetta could tell what his favorite foods were was by his love for reading food magazines. He'd flip through them once, study the pictures, and then that was it— he'd be done with the magazine but would store in his memory the pictures of the foods he wanted to try.

Chicken and French fries were Greg's favorite—he never failed to point to them on a menu at a restaurant. If there were no pictures of what he wanted, he still could find the chicken and fries choice and point to it, even if it were text.

When he didn't use his pad of paper to communicate, it was Arnetta's job to try to gauge what Greg was in the mood for. He rarely initiated activities, but Arnetta knew that Greg never said no to sports. Nereid hosted an annual Olympic event that Greg absolutely loved. So each time Arnetta asked him if was ready to practice, he didn't hesitate; he jetted for the door. For hours he would practice shooting baskets—but he'd just shoot the ball into the hoop and then wait for Arnetta to retrieve the ball. He also loved to go swimming in the pool at Nereid. Just as when I used to take him to the community pool, he'd do amazing flips and cannon balls into the pool—all with a straight face.

His practice and experience in the Olympic event at Nereid led Greg to try his hand at the Special Olympics—he ended up competing in sprinting, swimming, and gymnastics. I never would have thought that his odd habits of running back and forth, up and down the hallways of our apartments, and doing flips off the bunk beds, and terrorizing the kids at the community pool would lead him to two gold medals in gymnastics and swimming in the Special Olympics. I don't know if these accomplishments had anything to do with Arnetta's being in Greg's life, but he was enjoying things he'd never enjoyed before.

Greg's world began to open up in new ways. Arnetta started to take Greg on day excursions, often traveling throughout the city by public transit. He was very independent when the two of them went out together, taking care of such tasks as putting his money in the fare machine and walking to the back of the bus to sit down. They would even go to the movies at times. He'd stay focused on the story in the film the entire time, but if he didn't like the movie, he'd try to leave, or he'd glance around the theater aimlessly or shut his eyes.

Greg's being with Arnetta became so natural for the two of them that Arnetta began to bring him to her home. Trips to Arnetta's home became such a common occurrence that Greg developed a lifelong bond with her children. He became part of her family, and her children wanted to communicate with him. Eventually, Greg taught the whole family sign language, passing on his valuable lessons from Cheshire.

Over the years, Arnetta became my new contact person, the one I would talk to most about Greg's progress. It was nice to have a personal evaluation of my son, as opposed to the formal evaluations given by a state administrator. It was much more gratifying to have a telephone conversation about Greg instead of receiving the same form letter year after year. Arnetta and I grew to like each other and began to have conversations over the phone, and during my visits with Greg, we would discuss our challenges and rewards of mothering boys. We both shared the common path of raising young black men in today's society, one that is filled with the temptation of drugs and crime. It was a relief for her to hear me talking about my experiences raising my children and making it to the other side of the struggle. Each of my boys—except for Greg, of course—had to deal with addiction or jail or both at one time in their lives. It was good for Arnetta to know that if mine could get through it, so could hers. She was comforted when I would tell her, "Boys will run you crazy, but you will get through it. If I did, you can, too."

My family and I think Arnetta is a phenomenal person—she has treated Greg like a member of her own family. We are amazed and appreciative that she took on this kind of responsibility and shared such love for somebody else's child. I consider this amazing woman my eldest daughter. I call her my darling and my angel sent from God. It was preordained that we should meet.

CHAPTER SEVENTEEN

Atlanta

When he saw my sister for the first time after he moved from New York, he signed the word "aunt." It warmed my heart that he was so comfortable after being away from us for so long.

Due to the extraordinary levels of success that my nephew Tupac reached during his brief music career and because of the way that my sister handled his business affairs after his murder in 1996, we all went from living in tenement apartments to being homeowners. I was finally able to provide for my family in ways I had never been able to before. And most important, I was able to consider bringing Greg to Atlanta.

Greg was already scheduled to come for my daughter, Jamala's, wedding. I thought it would be a good opportunity to see how he adjusted in a new environment, one that could possibly become a permanent one.

Arnetta and Greg drove from New York to Atlanta. It was going to be a special day for the entire family. I knew that Jamala's wedding day would be perfect if I had all of my children together in one place.

And perfect it was. It turned out to be one of the most memorable days in the recent history of our family. It was a day of emotion. A day of triumph. Our family had been through so much together, but this was a sort of a culmination of the past, of all we'd endured. To see all of my children together as adults, standing at the altar, with Jamala in her wedding dress and each of my boys in their suits, filled my emotions like never before.

It was the first time that Greg's brothers had seen him in years. I was so touched when my second eldest, Scott, leaned over and said to me, "Wow, look at what he's become. He's a more peaceful soul now. He has the same old idiosyncrasies, but Ma, he's very peaceful."

Having Greg in Atlanta with us that week made me realize that I wanted him home with the family. I missed our visits. I wasn't able to spend time with him as often as I had since I moved to Atlanta, and I wanted to see him more. The dilemma of whether or not to pull him out of Nereid and away from Arnetta was no longer a question. I knew what I wanted.

I decided to share my thoughts with Arnetta about possibly re-locating Greg. And without hesitation, she said to me, "Can I come with him? I will move there." I couldn't believe it. This was all I needed to hear. I had no plan in place, but I knew I had to make it happen. It was time.

In addition to the house that Tom and I lived in, we owned a second home that was completely paid off. My oldest, Billy, was living in it, having recently separated from his wife. After I was able to persuade him to go back to her, it opened up for Arnetta and Greg. I jumped at the opportunity. From one conversation with Arnetta in May, it progressed to the journey that would take the two of them from New York to Atlanta that August.

Just three months after I spoke the words aloud to Arnetta that I wanted Greg to move to Atlanta, Arnetta and her entire family moved Greg into the house less than a mile away from me.

My concerns about moving him out of an environment that he'd become accustomed to were gone when Arnetta told me what

Greg had done. As soon as she mentioned going back to Atlanta after their first visit, he immediately packed his belongings—the pictures on the wall, everything. He was ready to go. This was his way of saying that he was finished with Nereid and ready to move closer to his family.

Arnetta gave up her paycheck from Nereid to move to Atlanta to take care of Greg. Though I did give her a home to live in, she would no longer be receiving a paycheck. She was fine with that because she loved Greg. She loved our family. And my family loved her. By extension, I consider Arnetta, her husband, and her children part of my family. She saw this as a new beginning for herself.

Greg acclimated to his surroundings in Atlanta just fine and very quickly. It was as if he hadn't been away for long at all. When he saw my sister for the first time after he moved from New York, he signed the word "aunt." It warmed my heart that he was so comfortable after being away from us for so long.

Today, it works out wonderfully that Greg's living around the corner from me, with Arnetta and within walking distance. There couldn't be a better situation for all of us. Arnetta tells me that sometimes Greg will sign the word for "mother" to let her know he wants to visit. He gets dressed, matches everything perfectly, brushes his teeth, sprays on some cologne, and excitedly stands by the door.

Greg's life in Atlanta has turned out to be equally as fulfilling for him as it has for us. He can attend church with us on Sundays, and we are able to enjoy his presence at all the family events. Our living within blocks of each other and having Arnetta as his primary caretaker made everything move smoothly for him. When he comes to the family functions, he even dances. At a recent holiday event at my youngest son, Katari's, house, Greg actually got up and danced with a family friend. The two danced together while family and friends egged him on, "Go, Greg! Go, Greg!" He was in the moment, feeling the comfort of his family, feeling as though he was home.

A few weeks later, we pulled up at Katari's home again. I saw Greg's face light up. He couldn't wait to get out of the car. He just knew that there was another dance party inside. When he walked in the house and found Katari and others engrossed in an NBA game, his expression melted—no dancing, only a boring basketball game. Greg took a seat in the background and sighed.

It was interesting to note that as a young boy, when Greg heard music, he would just jump. He'd sometimes rock, but mostly he'd jump up and down—fast. Jumping was also one of his movements that he used for self-stimulation. But now, as I watch him dance, I think to myself, *He's really in it—dancing and even dancing* with *someone!*

Billy, Scott, Kenny, Katari, and Jamala each have their own children now, so it's nice that their kids get to spend time with Greg. I believe that it's good for them to know their uncle with autism, instead of just knowing that they have an uncle somewhere who is always talked about but never seen. When they talk to children in their schools who have autism, they can say, "Our uncle has autism too."

CHAPTER EIGHTEEN

Finally, Home

It was in this moment I realized that I had made it. I made it through the hard part, through the confusion and fear. I had made it through the fog.

After Greg's fortieth birthday party was over and everyone had left my home, he stayed with me for the rest of the evening. I asked him if he wanted to lie down for a little while. He followed me into the bedroom and took his shoes off and turned on the television. I checked on him a few minutes later and noticed he had fallen asleep.

Arnetta and her daughter came to pick up Greg a few hours later. When they walked in the house, Greg's face lit up. The moment they walked through the door, he was so happy that he never looked my way again. As they left, Greg waved one of his quick salute waves, but he did not look at me once as he walked out the door. As the car pulled away, I watched until I couldn't see them anymore.

In that moment, forty years of memories flashed through my mind—the frustrations, the challenges, the hardships; the smiles, the laughter, and the tears. Despite the obstacles, my family and I stuck together and got through all that life presented us. And for this, I was so grateful for them—for my children, for my sister, Afeni, and her children, and for Tom, who had passed away a year earlier. It was each of them who took this journey of raising Greg with me. It was each of them who stood by me through the hardest decisions that I, as a mother, ever had to make; each of them who helped me on my journey down this road.

It was in this moment that I realized that I had made it. I made it through the hard part, through the confusion and fear. I had made it through the fog.

I was standing in the light at the end of the tunnel. I felt a peacefulness come over me. I was happy again.

Greg and Set

Greg and Gloria

Greg and Billy